MW01010650

# 7 Techniques to Open Your Third Eye Chakra

## *Fast and Simple Techniques to Increase Awareness and Consciousness*

Andrew Black

# © Copyright 2016 Andrew Black- All rights reserved.

The contents of this book may not be reproduced, duplicated or transmitted without direct written permission from the author.

Under no circumstances will any legal responsibility or blame be held against the publisher for any reparation, damages, or monetary loss due to the information herein, either directly or indirectly.

## Legal Notice:

This book is copyright protected. This is only for personal use. You cannot amend, distribute, sell, use, quote or paraphrase any part or the content within this book without the consent of the author.

## Disclaimer Notice:

Please note the information contained within this document is for educational and entertainment purposes only. Every attempt has been made to provide accurate, up to date and reliable complete information. No warranties of any kind are expressed or implied. Readers acknowledge that the author is not engaging in the rendering of legal, financial, medical or professional advice. The content of this book has been derived from various sources. Please consult a licensed professional before attempting any techniques outlined in this book.

By reading this document, the reader agrees that under no circumstances are is the author responsible for any losses, direct or indirect, which are incurred as a result of the use of information contained within this document, including, but not limited to, —errors, omissions, or inaccuracies.

# Table of Contents

# Introduction

You have probably heard of the Third Eye Chakra but have never really understood what it is. This book goes into detail giving you methods that have worked and that will help you toward being able to open the Third Eye and understand its significance. There are many different versions of what happens when you do and it's no wonder that people get confused about it. Following my own experience, I thought that the best way of addressing these differences was to add my own take on how to open the Third Eye and let you, the reader, benefit from my experience as this may also align with your activities and your beliefs and that seems to be important.

The human brain is a wonderful machine, but we are far from understanding all of the power that it possesses. In Hinduism, the Third Eye chakra opening is a revelation as it is in Buddhism, although it is referred to as Enlightenment in the latter. Those who are enlightened, such as the original Buddha are those who have found answers that normal means would not allow them to find. When you see contemplative monks on the Tibetan hills outside of temples, this is the enlightenment that they seek. They call it Nirvana, which is a place where all things become crystal clear. To Hindus, it is very much the same though thought of in slightly different terms as opening the Third Eye Chakra.

As you go through this book, you will be shown exercises that help to lead you to opening this Third Eye chakra and gaining a greater understanding of what you see when you look inward and what you see when you look outward. Remember, humans are limited by what they know and when they step beyond this, it is very hard to grasp what is happening, though those who are able to open the Third Eye are indeed enlightened and can see so much. The problem then is explaining to people who do not have this enlightenment how it is achieved and this is the purpose of this book.

It offers no guarantees since everyone's individual approach will dictate whether they are able to open their Third Eye Chakra. However, since the methods shared in this book have been tested, it is really down to the individual to get beyond their own prejudices and doubts that get in the way of being able to understand. This is my story and I am sharing it with you because you deserve to know what your brain is capable of doing, but you also deserve to learn what it takes to actually do what is required. You will never open the Third Eye Chakra with skepticism. You must believe and you must work toward the kind of enlightenment and total trust that is part of the experience.

# Chapter 1 – What is the Third Eye?

I have seen many explanations of this but the most accurate is that the Third Eye is something that is located between your eyebrows. Place your finger at the top of your nose and up a little until you get to that point where your eyebrows would join and this is the area where the third eye is located. It is not an eye in the natural sense and certainly does not look like one, but it is able to discern certain truths and can observe spiritual development as well as being able to make the brain see things in a different way than traditional eyes can.

Scientifically, we know that this area is the area of the brain that has the label of Pineal gland. You may have heard of serotonin – which is a feel good hormone produced by the pineal gland in the form of melatonin. If you understand the shape of the skull, this pinecone shaped gland is located just as we have indicated above and is responsible for many feelings of euphoria, although people such as Rene Descartes described it as being where the soul of man is located. You may not be aware of its existence at this moment in time, but that's because it's a relatively small gland, being about the size of a grain of rice although the impact it can have on your life can be mind-blowing.

The third eye is associated with spirituality and understanding of spiritual things. Many people mistake this for being religious, although one can be religious without being spiritual. For example, many people in the teachings of the church while not believing in spirituality being with you at all times. When the third eye is opened, it changes your life and your perspective of things and you have this feeling of inner wellbeing that you may never have otherwise experienced. It's almost akin to the opening of a door to understanding.

We know that in Hinduism, there are chakras through the body that allow energy flow and that many of the exercises that are performed by yoga classes help to open up this energy flow. There are also consequences to blockages of any of the Chakras, though to many people, the Third Eye Chakra remains a mystery, because they cannot step beyond the worldly beliefs that they hold into the spiritual plane required to open the third eye to greater understanding.

The third eye sees things as if witnessing them and those

things that are witnessed allow the individual to feel closer to understanding the spiritual world as well as being able to gain a better understanding of mindfulness. It looks inward as well as outward and sees many things that in normal terms are hard to describe. We already have an understanding from our physical lives, for example, of what good and bad is and are able to distinguish such things as black and white, bright and dim, etc., but the third eye sees much more than this and with a clarity that can be a little startling at first because enlightenment of any kind goes beyond the normal understanding that humans grow up with. It goes beyond right and wrong and thus teaching about the Third eye to those with little understanding can seem a little far-fetched or place obstacles in the way of actually opening that third eye.

If you think of other glands within the body, their purpose is relatively simple to understand. There are physiological reasons why they exist and an explanation of their purpose and how the body feels when they do what they are supposed to do is simple to grasp. However, the Pineal gland differs from this, in that what you can experience using it may be feelings and emotions that you have not previously experienced. You may even experience seeing images or light that others cannot see. This is all a part of your experience and is individual to you. There are common elements that people have explained but the activity of the third eye defies exact scientific explanation. One may associate the seeing of colors with the activity of the third eye. Another may describe it as crystal clear thoughts, though we know that either of these can be achieved without the use of the pineal gland. What makes the difference is that the clarity defies description and the colors seen are almost unworldly.

In brief, the Third Eye is like a bridge between this physical world that we live in and the spiritual divide. Opening of the Third eye allows you to see more and to use more of your brain than perhaps you have been able to use in the past. I am able to distinguish colors surrounding the objects that I see that give them more clarity of meaning. I am also able to reach those stimuli that touch spiritual belief and nearness to what one may describe as total understanding.

Everyone will see their own opening of the Third Eye differently and those who have experienced it will be humble in their explanation because it's larger than one can easily describe. There is no ego attached to the attainment of this kind of understanding. In fact, ego may even get in the way of ever being able to see through the Third eye, since what is seen is hard to quantify in a way that people can relate to.

I think that the best words to use to describe the activity of the third eye are "total spiritual understanding and acceptance" or the word "glory" because these human descriptions will help you to see the benefits of using the exercises in this book to attempt to begin your own journey and your own discovery of what the Pineal Gland or third eye is to you.

# Chapter 2 – Third Eye Benefits

If you have ever questioned the purpose of life, then the Third eye has benefits for you that will take you beyond your normal understanding of life. You will no longer question the purpose because you will instinctively know that the purpose is larger than you are and that you are simply a vessel to carry life from one era to another. That may sound strange, but when you are able to believe in a higher power and see yourself in terms of being small, you appreciate more about what's going on around you and are able to discern so much more because you have put ego out of the picture.

I first discovered this when I was faced with the beauty of creation. You may have experienced seeing something stunningly beautiful that takes your breath away. In that moment of clarity, you understand the wonder of life and you also understand that it's bigger than any human thought ever could be. The tingle at the back of your neck or the feeling of calm that encompasses you is because you have become smaller than that which you are experiencing. Your third eye is allowing you to see beyond the physical or what your eyes see. You feel the presence of something spiritual that you cannot describe but that you know makes you feel completely whole.

The third eye is the area of the brain that is responsible for intuition and many put intuition to one side, thinking that perhaps it is going to be scorned or not taken seriously. However, the kind of intuitive feeling that you get when you open your Third eye leaves no room for doubt. You know that your intuition is right and that it comes from somewhere other than simple logic can explain. Thus, there is no ego attached to it.

When you open your third eye, you are able to trust yourself in a way that you may never have previously trusted yourself. You find more inner strength to do things that you may not have been able to do in the past. The power of sixth sense belongs to the Third eye and you can imagine that when you are able to tap into this, it makes you a very powerful thinker and able to do much good with what you learn.

In fact, everything that a human being needs to know or may question is answered by the Third eye. We just need to be able to tap into that information and most people can't because they are too busy doing whatever it is that they do to get through life. However, you can learn to develop the use of the third eye in your spare time by learning the benefits of chant and of meditation. In that moment of meditation, you step away from your busy world and give the third eye its chance to shine. Of course, it won't happen without training, but when you are able to do this, you will know instinctively if something is right or wrong and won't need other people to validate your thought. You may think things you are unaccustomed to thinking and find that you can predict events or place yourself on the same wavelength as someone who is miles away.

You shift your understanding of life to a higher plane and thus you benefit from having a greater understanding than otherwise everyday limiting belief. You learn not to stress the small stuff in life because as your opening of the third eye happens, you are able to see answers clearly that help            you            to            move            forward.

The wisdom that you gain will startle you at first and it takes you a little while to actually recognize it for what it is. People are used to questioning their own decisions or ideas but when you are able to use the third eye and recognize what it is, your doubts will be something of the past and you will make decisions based on amazingly accurate assessment of a situation. Your third eye knows how to heal you from illnesses. It knows how to manifest great relationships and is used for all kinds of benefits in your life that you may not have anticipated.

You are more likely to find that the Law of Attraction works in your favor because the clarity that you "see" through the third eye allows you to put doubts to one side and to work toward all of the things you want to achieve within the course of a lifetime. Does this mean you can use it as a powerful tool against others? That is not its purpose, nor is it the purpose of the Third eye to allow you to have a greater ego. You need to start to understand how the third eye works because it isn't about ego at all. It's about knowing and being sure and seeing things in a much clearer way that helps you to take whatever is the "right" path forward.

When Siddhartha Gautama meditated to try and find the answer to mankind's suffering, there was no ego involved. He was not trying to be famous. He was not trying to inflate his own ego. He humbly put himself into that space where the third eye informs. He had the right questions and received the right answers. In fact, they were so right that Buddhist philosophy is centered upon what he discovered four centuries before the birth of Christ and is as relevant today as it was then. It's astounding what benefits you gain from opening the third eye, but your approach will determine whether you are able to do this or will fail.

# Chapter 3 – Technique 1

You need to have a good sound experience of meditation to open the Third Eye. This may mean that you take a yoga class and work under the instruction of an expert, or you may be fortunate enough to be able to share the way forward that was offered to me. If you can find a retreat that offers people the help of a Guru, this is very useful in the learning of meditation. Meditation isn't simply sitting thinking of nothing. It's a lot more complex than that. It's something that needs to become a daily event and many people give up because they have no real understanding of what it is they are trying to achieve or why it helps in opening the third eye. Let me try to explain from a simply perspective in the best way that I know how.

Beautiful things created by nature surround us and yet you probably walk past them every day of your life without taking inspiration from them. Your eyes concentrate on your driving or on the plans for today's work and you continue to walk through your life without actually sensing much that is spiritual. You may occasionally glance at something you find enchanting and it may even take your breath away, but in our everyday lives, this is a rarity.

The reason I bring this up is that before you can meditate to any great extent, you need to be happy in the skin you are in and you can't do that without humility. If you try, you fail miserably because you are letting your own expectations get in the way of what you are potentially going to gain. When you talk to people who meditate for the first time, they are skeptical. They know that thoughts invaded when they were supposed to simply concentrate on breathing. They didn't know how to stop them and they come up with all sorts of excuses such as "Meditation didn't work for me."

The problem with approaching meditation with expectations is that you are not letting go of the human values of "what's in it for me?" and the third eye powers don't work like that. The reason that I mention nature is for a very specific purpose. Before you take up meditation, you need to experience humility and smallness, so that what happens to you during meditation comes as a blessing that you can appreciate. Go to a beauty spot at either sunset or sunrise and open your eyes to spiritual possibility before you go onto the next technique, which is meditation.

Sit down and appreciate what you are surrounded with and the more awe this brings out in you, the better. I chose a spot in the middle of the moorlands and there is a church high up on a hill that gives me a view of all of the moorlands around that high point. From this point of beauty, I instantly know my place in life and feel small in comparison with everything I see. It humbles me and reminds me of my own fragility but it does much more than that.

In order to receive the gifts that the third eye gives you, you have to have been in this position of awe at everything you see around you, to such an extent that you see everything in perspective. You are as small as a grain of sand and as you look into the distance, you can see hills and valleys, trees and sky and know that the universe is a wondrous place that you are honored to be able to be part of.

As you sit there, breathe in through the nose and hold the breath for a moment. It's important that your body is sitting straight and that your backbone is indeed in a straight posture, so that your breathing pivots your upper abdomen and you feel the rush of air into your body. Let it linger a moment and then breathe out. Continue to breathe in this way as you observe the world around you and soak in its beauty. It is necessary to know your spiritual side and this technique allows you to get up close and personal with spirituality. Do not think of worldly things. Simple observe the world as it presents itself and see yourself as a small pebble or grain of sand, but know above all else that you are part of this wonderful scene and that the part you play in it is in harmony with everything that you are seeing.

If you continue to breathe in this way and can put all thought out of your mind, you are beginning to feel the opening of the third eye to spirituality, inner understanding and appreciation of life itself. Don't expect anything. Simply be satisfied that you have understood your humility as the rest comes as a consequence of discipline. Placing yourself into a wonderful environment such as this and trusting in your mind to be able to see beyond the reality of what's in front of you is your first step toward allowing the Third eye to start to open. Trust your intuition as you enjoy the scene. Trust your inner faith and know that you accept who you are.

You may be more inspired by the coastline and this works too. You need to place yourself in line with nature and become part of it without expectations of any kind of reward. If you expect reward, most likely, you haven't experienced humility at its best and you need to let go of worldly things to achieve this perfect peace. I have put this as a priority because you can't step from a commercial and very competitive world into meditation very easily until you have understood this part of the process. Now that you have, you are beginning to see how the Third eye works and what you need to do in order to achieve better understanding of its function and its purpose to your life.

# Chapter 4 – Technique 2

You have learned in the previous chapter about the good approach to meditation, although we have not covered the ability to meditate and this is vital to opening the Third eye chakra. In fact, meditation does not guarantee that this will happen. However, if you have done the previous exercise, you are ready for meditation because you already understand the benefits of breathing correctly and holding your posture so that your back is straight, allowing the energy to pass through the other chakras located in other parts of the body.

Technique two is about embracing the idea of meditation and making it part of your daily routine. If you are able to join a yoga class run by an experienced teacher, this will help you. My own personal experience was in the company of a guru who was able to put forward his ideas about what meditation was all about. I feel honored to have learned with his help. The automatic thing for the mind to do when you sit still is to think. Meditation replaces random thought with specific concentration on the energy flowing into the body while breathing.

## Ambiance

It's a good idea to have a quiet area for your meditation. I chose my room and had a section devoted to meditation. I placed items such as a Buddha statue and inspirations objects into this area and you can do the same. If you are someone who enjoys essential oils, having a diffuser in the area with a wonderfully inspirational aroma can help you. Some people prefer to have incense sticks. Remember, if you form an altar, you are not expected to worship any of the pieces that you choose to place on the altar. It isn't like a church. The altar is merely used for items that inspire you. I use a photograph of a Buddhist priest because the scenery and the color do inspire me enormously.

## Position

It is not obligatory to sit in a full lotus pose and in fact this may cause difficulty for beginners. However, if you have a hard cushion and sit on it, bend your knees and cross your ankles. Then sway left and right until you feel perfectly balanced. Place your strongest hand onto your lap palm upward and then place the other hand into it the same way up. If you are unable to sit on a cushion, you can meditate on a hard chair, as long as you use the rules that your feet are flat on the floor, your back is straight and you feel centered. You will also place your hands on your lap as instructed before.

Empty your mind. The thoughts that you are permitted to think while you are meditating are clear. You imagine the air going in through your nostrils and feel it enter your body to the count of seven. You hold your breath to the count of five and then exhale to the count of eight. You can see by this that meditation gives your mind something to concentrate on to get you away from worldly thoughts. Follow the directions given below.

- Inhale through the nostrils to the count of seven.
- Hold onto the breath for the count of five,
- Exhale to the count of eight.
- Count one.
- Inhale through the nostrils to the count of seven,
- Hold onto the breath for the count of five.
- Exhale to the count of eight,
- Count two.

You can see that at the end of the exhale: count one, two,

three etc., and the idea is to get to the count of ten. In the early stages of meditation, don't expect to get this far without some thought invading your mind. Forgive yourself instantly and dismiss the thought, going back to one again.

You will find that meditation helps you to open the Third Eye, because you are giving your mind the peace that it needs in order to do that. It won't happen straight away and all of the Buddhist monks that meditate are aiming toward opening the Third Eye chakra to try and get to that place of total understanding that does just that. The more you practice your meditation, the better you will get at it. It took me about 4 weeks of meditation before I felt anything of this nature. Some people take even longer, but when you do feel that journey happening in your head, you are aware of it and when you stop meditating, the thoughts can stay with you for a long time. This intuitive opening up of spiritual thoughts is valuable to you are a human being and reaching this point with your meditation is the aim of the technique.

# Chapter 5 – Technique 3

Chanting is another way to jump start the pineal gland into action and there are very good reasons why this works. The actual vibration that chanting produces touches the bone within the nose called the tetrahedron bone. You can replace thinking about your breathing with chanting while you meditate, although it will take you a little while to drop the feeling of embarrassment that is perfectly normal when you start to do something that you are not accustomed to doing. The first time that I chanted, for example, I was given a chant that was specifically targeted to me, based on my birthdate and the hour of my birth. The words meant nothing to me, but that's okay because they are not meant to have a meaning that may make your thoughts start to build chains of other thoughts. The idea is that the chant replaces thought.

Of course when you chant, you need to get the chanting right and the instructions below will help you to do that. Since you may not be working with a guru as I was, use the standard chant of OM, which is pronounced A-U-M. The inhaling process is much the same as it is with other forms of meditation. This is always done through the nostrils. The difference comes, however, on the exhale. As you exhale, you will be chanting and this is done with the lips slightly apart so that you can feel a tingle sensation as you chant. Try it several times before going into meditation. Just breathe in and then chant on the outward breath.

As you inhale, straighten your back and allow the flow of energy to build up so that on the exhale you have sufficient breath to make the sound last. Many teachers get those who are unaccustomed to chanting to actually concentrate on breathing and then sing the musical scales to get them into the right frame of mind to chant. Then they introduce the A-U-M sound. You are told to let your energy out and send it upward when you are chanting and after a while this becomes quite automatic. You learn that you are the A-U-M rather than it being something that you are producing.

You may find it useful to have a Tibetan singing bowl although this is not necessary. What I find is that it helps set the mood and the tone for the chant. This is a bowl where you have a wooden tool that you rotate around the rim and it produces a singing note, a little like the Om that you are trying to produce. These come in various tones and the smaller they are, the higher the tone.

Remember that the sequence is always to breathe in and to sound the Om on the exhale until you find that you are following this rhythm naturally. The Om helps you to shut out external thoughts, but they may come into your head anyway. If they do, do not consider yourself a failure. Merely dismiss them and start again.

## Com Mediation

When you have the flow correct, start your meditation session. Breathe in, hold the breath for a moment and then chant on the out breath, being sure that the sound creates that tingle on your lips and that you put as much energy into it as you can. Westerners are always a little embarrassed by this at first, but once you get accustomed to it, you will not find this will deter you from doing it correctly.

During the course of the next twenty minutes, breathe in, hold the breath, breathe out and chant. Your mind can reach really high levels of enlightenment using this method and many find that the energy of the chant is what leads to the opening of the Third eye. Remember, it's not a physical eye although some report that when it happens, there is a slight feeling inside the head at the point where the chakra is located.

Remember that those who are truly enlightened will still feel the benefit of meditation long after the meditation has ceased, although this takes time. When you have finished meditation, you should always take your time getting back to the world because mediation lowers your heartbeat and your blood pressure. Use this time to record on paper what you can do next time you chant to make the session more successful. This noting your progress helps you considerably because instead of repeating the same exercise over and over, you are learning your own faults and flaws and picking up on them, so that next time, your meditation experience improves.

You will find that this method is very good for relaxation as well as for helping you to open the Third eye and if you gain nothing else from the meditation, you will gain relaxation and a sense of wellbeing.

# Chapter 6 – Technique 4

This technique calls for the use of crystals and these can be very powerful at opening up the Third eye. Tourmaline is a particularly good crystal to help to open up the Third eye and the way in which it is used will differ depending upon the user. Amethyst is also good and you can purchase these in wand format at a specialist crystal store. I would suggest when you try to use crystals that you learn to have a relaxation session before you start your crystal session to help you concentrate.

Place the tip of the wand on the place where the pineal gland is located and keep it there for about twenty minutes a day. What this purports to do is to clear up the calcification which may be stopping the pineal grand from working, but before you try this, you need to be in the right position because the direct sunlight on the crystal against your pineal gland is what is needed to activate the pineal gland.

I also found it powerful to use crystals hanging from the ceiling in the window of my bedroom and could sun gaze through them at any time that I chose to. Personally, it worked better when I was relaxed and as long as the sunlight passes through the crystal and hits the pineal gland, you will get results. I had to move the furniture around a bit in the bedroom to make sure that this happened but you can also use a yoga mat and a pillow rather than moving the furniture. There is a very surreal feeling when the pineal gland is activated. I found that this does not work on its own and that doing it in conjunction with meditation and relaxation was very necessary because this puts your mind into a more receptive mode so that you are more susceptible.

This should be done every couple of days but what happens is strangely bazaar. You begin to be more aware of colors and the spectrum of colors that you see as almost surreal. The colors carry on into your day and will help you to produce auras when you look at people and the color determines the character or the state of mind of the person you are viewing. This is also very accurate and you find that you can judge anger, lethargy, desperation and other emotions just by recognizing the color of the aura. For those who are not aware of what an aura is, this is a colored ring around people – a bit like a halo, but it extends around the whole body, rather than just being above the head. Different to a halo, the aura touches the body and changes as the person you are looking at changes the emotional state that he or she is in.

# Chapter 7 – Technique 5

Mindfulness is something that is becoming popular in this day and age, although it hales back to the time of the original Buddha. What it means is being able to be in the moment. Why this matters to being able to open the Third Eye is that if you have too many thoughts in your mind, you won't have the concentration that you need in order to open the Third Eye. Your head will be too stuffed full of the baggage you may have brought through your life and that doesn't help clarity of mind at all.

Mindfulness is something that you need to learn to practice in your life to get rid of negativity, as this negativity may just be what keeps your Third eye from opening. You cannot see the answer to all things if your mind is filled with too many thoughts.

Thus, mindful practice in conjunction with the other techniques we have mentioned will be useful to you. We have talked a little about intuition and when the Third eye is open, your intuitive qualities are very strong. Now, imagine what happens when your mind is clouded by a lot of other activities and thoughts, emotions and feelings; there is no clear passage for intuition.

Therefore practicing mindfulness becomes very important. The way that you practice mindfulness is to sit down and relax. Breathe as we have taught you in previous chapters and be aware of the exact moment you are in. Buddhists do this and it is very powerful once you are able to incorporate mindfulness into everything that you do. Think about it. If you are in the moment, you are able to gain everything from that moment and that includes intuitive power.

Thus, when you eat, be mindful. Take your time and enjoy every taste, aroma and texture of your food. When you clean a floor, put all that you are into the task and whenever your mind tries to go elsewhere, acknowledge the thought and then dismiss it. If you fill your mind with thoughts, intuition is very hard to switch on.

However, the Third eye becomes more active when you are mindful. I can give you an example of this. In my early days of working with my guru, I was asked to wash a floor. I was asked to consider the task the most important thing that I had to do in the world and to ignore thoughts about yesterday                     or                     tomorrow.

I wasn't sure what my guru was trying to teach me, but I did as I was asked, being totally mindful of every action I took and dismissing thoughts that wandered elsewhere. What I felt inside me when I totally put myself into that moment was a contentment that was indescribable, but it was a very peaceful feeling indeed, as if my mind was being taken to another place where peace exists.

I also found that I intuitively did things with a single mindedness and that I was able to achieve more by this means of doing things. My intuition has since been honed and I trust it entirely, whereby before this event, I would have questioned myself on numerous occasions instead of being this close to the feeling of knowing.

The Pineal gland opening or the Third Eye chakra opening is all about clarity and when you see it in this format you gain happiness inside you that you cannot gain from other means. You have to understand that this happens when you are not seeking it. You don't control the opening of the Third Eye chakra. This is something you feel happen as a result of your mindfulness and your humility and when it does happen, you are aware of it in a very positive manner.

# Chapter 8 – Technique 6

This chapter relates to the care you need to take of your chakras in general. This is important because if you ignore the whole chakra system throughout your body, you cannot expect the Third Eye chakra to respond to your wish for it to open. You need to look after yourself and make sure that you follow the advice given below.

## Yoga

Yoga will help you to keep all the energy flowing through your chakras. It targets certain areas of the body and will also help you to learn meditation in the presence of your instructor. Although I have given you an outline for meditation in this book, it always helps practically if you do enlist the help of a teacher, who may be able to show you how to open up your chakras by the different movements and how to achieve great meditation skills.

## The food that you eat

In this day and age, there is much pollution. If you allow pollution to enter your body, you also need to make sure that you take protective measures to make sure that your body is healthy at all times. Good quality food will help you and it's essential to start reading labels and to avoid all the chemical elements that are manmade and which may be contributing to health issues. A detox on a regular basis is also advised. I use nettle and the way this is used is to make a tea with it in a pan and then wait until it has cooled down and pour it into a water bottle, so that I can have cold drinks at any time of the day. This gives you water, but it also gives you a very powerful detox. Try to avoid fluoride in your diet and in your teeth cleaning procedures, as this is something that can be harmful to you.

**The exercise that you participate in**

You need to look after your body. Getting into a regular routine of exercise, no matter how simply this form of exercise is, will help you. Dance is a great exercise in more than one way. If you also sing at the same time as dancing, you help to free up the chakra which is located in the neck area and when this chakra is blocked, it's very unlikely that you will achieve good quality meditation or that you will be able to work toward opening the Third Eye.

## Breathing exercises

Although we have mentioned breathing in a former chapter, there are powerful methods of breathing that can help you in your quest. For example, alternate nostril breathing can help you to clear your mind and is very powerful. In this system of breathing, place your thumb over your right nostril and breathe in through the left nostril. Then while keeping the air inside your body, move the thumb over to the other nostril and breathe out. By alternating the nostrils, you are clearing the nasal passages and this helps considerably to sharpen your thoughts so that you are better able to concentrate.

## Activities to sharpen the mind

It helps sometimes to turn off the automatic nature of TV and try some activities that help you to keep your mind sharp. I would suggest such things as crossword puzzles, playing around with Luminosity on your tablet and actually doing a fair share of reading. This all helps to quiet the mind but also makes you think very logically and this helps you to hone the intuitive values of the Third Eye.

Taking care of your body and your lifestyle is really an obligation. You owe it to yourself to do this regardless of what you are looking for in life. If you are looking to open the Third Eye, it's unlikely that you will achieve it unless you look after yourself and take your life seriously. That doesn't mean you don't have time to enjoy yourself and benefit from laughter. Laugher is every bit as important as being responsible for the condition of your body and in fact helps the chakras to stay in alignment so that you are open to experiencing the opening of the Third eye when it happens.

# Chapter 9 – Technique 7

## *Following the Eightfold Path*

I believe that this gives you so much power and such a capacity for happiness that it becomes an essential part of understanding yourself and making the most of who you are. When you look at the Eightfold Path, this is the path that Buddhist Philosophy asks you to follow if you want to find happiness. It follows that this was a very important part of my journey toward opening the Third Eye. If your life is a shambles and you are unhappy with many aspects of it, it is very unlikely that you will have the concentration that you need to be able to come to that point of understanding the Third Eye Chakra gives you. Thus, it is my advice to readers to look into the eightfold path and see how near to achieving the behaviors and actions required under Buddhist philosophy.

The path consists of the following elements:

- Seeing things in the right way
- Having the right approach to letting go
- Being able to speak in the right way
- Being able to take the right action

- Being in the right job
- Putting in the right amount of energy
- Having complete awareness or mindfulness
- Being able to put in the right amount of concentration

Siddhartha Gautama formed the eightfold path as a result of his entering into Nirvana or having his Third Eye tell him why mankind suffered. It was his quest to find out why humans went through such pain in their lives and what he sensed through the Third Eye was that most people never fulfilled their quota of happiness because they went again the principles laid out above and in fact most of their suffering was self-inflicted.

It is worthwhile reading a full book on the eightfold path because the subject is very deep indeed and this chapter could not do it justice. However, in a nutshell, if you can adhere to the above rules, you will find yourself nearer to finding the bliss that happens when you open your Third Eye Chakra.

How it applied in my case was that I needed to look at my own weaknesses and strengthen them. For example, I have to admit that sometimes I didn't say the right thing, or didn't give sufficient concentration to things that I set out to do. I was in a job that did not give me any sense of happiness and could not let go of the past.

Read through the list and learn the list by heart and apply it to your life. If you use the other chapters of this book to help guide you, you will already have learned many of the rules, but self-discipline, mindfulness, being aware of others and learning to be true to who you are matter as well. Learning to interact with other human beings in a decent way also matters, which is why I started this book with humility. When you feel you are more important than others, you lose the ability to take all of the benefits of humility and these are essential.

Basically the premise of the Buddhist philosophy is to make people around you happy and to find true happiness that lasts within the person that you are. Too many people are lost in the past or worried about the future and don't notice their bad treatment of others.

If you truly want to open up the Third Eye chakra, you need to improve who you are to the maximum of your ability. That doesn't mean getting richer. In fact it has nothing whatsoever to do with material goodness. It's all about developing your own personality and the way that you interact with those around you. When you learn this, through the eightfold path, you are well on your way to experiencing the opening of the Third Eye.

It is merely a matter of adjusting your life. Everyone has this ability.

# Chapter 10 - The Secrets of Third Eye Activation

If you have read thus far, you will know that the secrets to Third Eye activation lie in the pages of this book. For each individual this will mean different things. They will need to make different changes to their lives depending upon where their lives are at the time of starting.

You cannot put hard and fast rules upon what it takes to activate your Third Eye. You can, however glean from those who have that certain actions in life make that opening more possible. These include:

- Being sufficiently humble
- Learning to be spiritual
- Learning to Meditate
- Learning to use Mindfulness as part of your daily existence
- Learning to breathe in the correct way
- Respecting your body and your mind
- Being able to follow the eightfold path
- Being patient and learning to understand your own spirituality

- Learning to accept others

All of these are important, and that's where the secret lies. One action will not make it happen, nor will expecting answers when you want them. You have to work toward that perfection that allows the Third eye to open. This book has shown you how based on real experience. Now, it's left for you to put the pieces together according to where you find yourself in life and begin to take the journey toward happiness and enlightenment.

# Chapter 11- Activating your Third Eye through Simple Exercises

A few simple exercises will help you in activating your third eye, which is related to your sixth chakra – the psychic chakra. It is located between your eyebrows, in the middle of the forehead; it's the place where your body and mind meet.

These exercises are aimed at connecting your body to your mind so that you can reap the benefits of opening your third eye. You should be careful while performing these exercises, as they are very advanced and can hurt you if not done properly.

### Exercise 1

This exercise is done with the help of a specific chant and with a particular tone. You only have to do it for three days, and its impact will be retained by your body, permanently.

The mantra that we will be using is "Thoh," it's

pronounced as "Toe." The tone should be just right- not high-pitched and not too deep, in between. It's not difficult to find the correct tone, just practice a little and you'll feel it when you hit the right tone. If you are not sure or have doubts then don't worry as long as you feel comfortable with the tone, it will work.

**Steps**

1. Sit down in a comfortable area and make sure that your back is straight. If you can't keep your back straight then sit with some support then sitting with the support of a wall is the most effective.

2. Take a deep breath through your nose and then continue to hold your breath. You have to hold your breath as long, as it is comfortable; don't overstress yourself and even if it's only a small amount of time, it's fine. While holding your breath, open your mouth just a little so that your upper and lower teeth are parted. Then, take the tip of your tongue and place it between the gaps between your teeth. The tip of your tongue should touch your upper and lower teeth.

3. Start pressing the tip of your tongue with your teeth. Be gentle and don't use too much pressure. Now, release your breath but through your mouth in one exhale but slowly. While you are doing this chant the mantra, which is 'THOH'; drag the word as much as possible while you're exhaling so that it sounds like 'T-O-O-O-E-E-E.' Say the word only once every time that you exhale and continue to repeat this. The aim is to make your tongue vibrate while you're doing this; this is done with the help of the air that is passing out of your mouth. Try to feel the air that is moving out of your mouth while it is touching your teeth and tongue.

4. You have to repeat this activity five times in a row without stopping. You should practice a little before so that you are accustomed to the exercise and can perform five times without interruption.

5. You have to repeat this activity for three days. It should be done at the same time every day; the exercise should be performed twenty-four hours apart, always.

### Exercise 2

The second exercise should only be performed by those

who have done the first exercise. You have to wait ten to fourteen days before you can perform the second exercise or it won't be effective. The wait is important because your body needs some time to adapt to this new awakening and for the energy in your body to start flowing.

This exercise is different from the first one because it has euphoric effects. It will make you feel good and help in elevating your mood. Hence, it should only be done once a week as the effects last for a long time and you won't need to perform it more than once in a week.

1. Take a deep breath and hold your breath for exactly five seconds or you can simply count till five and then release your breath. You have to repeat this activity three times because it helps your body to relax and stay focused.

2. Now, you have to focus your attention on your third eye; do this by feeling and paying attention to the spot where your third eye is. The impact that you will feel is that you will be a little more aware of the spot where your third eye is, or you might even feel some pressure on that spot.

3. Take a deep breath again and hold it just like you did while doing exercise 1. You don't have to hold it in for a long time and just release your breath as soon as you start feeling a little uncomfortable. While you are releasing your breath chant the word "May" – the pronunciation is similar to that of the month May. The word should come out in one go, like this – "M-a-a-a-a-ay"; do this slowly and don't say it all in just one go, drag it as much as possible. The tone should be the same as exercise 1, not too high and not too low, just in between. It's okay to adjust your tone a little and change it while you're doing the exercise, it won't cause any problems. You just have to find the right pitch, and when you do, you'll just know.

4. Take a deep breath again and continue to do the same exercise five times in a row. While you are doing this activity, it's important to feel the energy that is going through your head and converging on your third eye. You can enjoy the effects of this energy by focusing on different parts of your head where the energy travels- your forehead, then the middle of your brain and lastly, your third eye.

This is what makes this exercise so blissful, and by focusing on the energy, you are ensuring that it has a lasting impact on your body. You will feel a little light after doing this exercise, but it will pass after a few minutes. You might feel similar sensations causing euphoria later on during the next one week at any point in time.

# Chapter 12- Seven Things You Can Do To Sharpen Your Psychic Abilities

It's difficult to sharpen your psychic abilities and enhance your third eye when you don't exactly know what to do. This section of the book will tell you seven simple things that you can do daily to enhance your psychic powers. These tricks will help your intuition and mediumship abilities, get them going and make them grow.

There is no particular order that you have to perform these exercises in nor are they dangerous in any manner. They are simple and won't even take a lot of your time; just do them daily, and in no time you will feel your psychic abilities enhancing.

## Meditate

The main aim of meditation is to increase your vibration so that you can be in sync with the plane that governs your psychic abilities. Your spirit energy is what governs your psychic abilities, and it vibrates at a higher frequency than your body. If you want to develop your psychic abilities, then you have to get in sync with your spirit energy by meditating and increasing your vibration.

Meditation allows you to relax and focus; it's rather difficult to vibrate in sync with your spirit when you can't focus your attention. If you are in a relaxed state, then you can slowly increase your energetic vibration. You will feel the effect of meditation as you slowly feel elevated, connected to your spirit energy, your higher self and also the energy of others. Meditation is all about patience; learning to meditate effectively is important, and it only comes with continuous practice.

**Practice Psychometry**

Psychometry means learning to read the energy of an object and enhancing your psychic powers in the process. It's fun, and it won't feel like work at all; it's a great way to increase your abilities, in particular for beginners. All you have to is to find an object and hold onto it; the object should be something of significance that has lots of energy attached to it. It should preferably be made of metal because it's easier to channel energy through metal, like a wedding ring. Now, close your eyes and focus all of your attention on the object. Your goal is to sense something about the owner of the object by using your intuition; you might hear something or even see something if you tap into your intuitive sense.

## Walking in nature

Meditation is not something which is supposed to be boring, but that's what a lot of people think which is why they don't like to do it. You can meditate using a lot of ways and not just by sitting down and chanting. The most efficient way to meditate in an interesting way is by taking an intuitive walk in nature.

The walk isn't supposed to be just walking without thinking or doing anything; you have to stay mindful of your surroundings and what you are doing. Firstly, focus on the movement of your body and when you take a step say the word 'step' with it. The aim of this is to clear your mind of random thoughts and help increase your vibration.

If you don't want to concentrate on anything while you're walking, then there is no harm in that either. You can just walk ideally without paying attention to anything if you want and even that will be helpful.

## Know Your Spirit Guides

Spirit guides can be anything. They can be the souls of the people around you or of those who are dead. They are simply things that live in the spiritual world and can be used to harness your energy.

You should get to know your spirit guides so that they can help you understand and enhance your power. Asking them to show themselves during meditation can do this; you should ask them questions and get to know them. The more in contact you are with your spirit guides, the more you'll get in touch with your psychic abilities.

## Make a Symbol Book

Psychic intuiting and energy come to us in many ways, but the major medium is symbols that represent energy in metaphorical ways. Just buy a new journal and pen and sit down in a quiet environment.

Now, invite your spirit guides in to help you; you can do this by meditating. You should ask them to give you symbols for events that might happen or other things of importance. You should remember that symbols don't mean what they seem like, so don't take them literally, like a cake could mean birthday or you might even hear a birthday song. Write down the symbol that you saw in your book and what it meant to you.

**Seeing Auras**

An excellent way to develop your psychic abilities is to learn to see auras; anyone can learn to see auras because it's simple. Ask a friend to help you out and get them to stand in front of a plain colored wall; you have to step back about eight feet from them.

Now, focus on your friend's forehead in the area between the eyebrows where the third eye rests. You have to imagine as if you are looking through them at the wall behind and soon you will be able to see the aura layer around their head.

**Use Your Pet**

Including pets is a fun way to developing your psychic abilities because you can enjoy some time with your pet while trying to read them. Animals are beings that have comprehensive thoughts except we can't understand them but if you try you can pick up on how they are feeling.

Go to your pet when they are calm, sit with them; try to sense what they are feeling by using your intuition. The closer you are to your pet the more efficient this will be.

# Chapter 13- How to Identify and Make Use of Aura Colors

Every living thing emits an aura, which is a large energetic magnetic field around it. This magnetic field can be sensed, felt and even seen if you know how. It's pretty simple because you can always tell when someone is angry or sad by sensing the aura around him or her. Even without knowing how to read a person's aura you can tell how they feel when you get in touch with their aura.

## Identifying Aura Colors

This technique will help you to identify your aura, and it can be used to sense the aura of other people, too. Find a mirror and stand or sit several feet away from it and make sure that your background is solid and light colored.

Now, focus your attention on a single part of your body, it can be anything, but it's better to look at a place that has a lot of energy, which is the area between your eyebrows. You will soon start seeing a white-transparent image around your body; it might not be clear or definitive, but you will see it.

Continue to focus, and the white transparent image will soon start expanding and become stable. It then changes and represents a solid color; now, your mind is seeing something that it has not seen before and it's not prepared for it. So, the aura will disappear as your mind gets distracted and starts thinking.

This will continue to happen, and you will only see the aura for a few seconds before it disappears. The key is to remain focused long enough to not how your aura looks and what color it is; the more focused you are, the brighter the aura will become.

## Making Use of Aura Colors

You can make use of the aura colors by understanding the meaning behind them. Every person has a different aura that represents who that person is, the experiences they have gone through and their life force.

So, if you understand the meaning behind different aura colors, you can use it to understand people better. You can even find the meaning behind your aura and know yourself better. It helps you to get in sync with your spirit energy and your higher self.

The following are the different aura colors and what kind of people they represent:

**Red Aura:** Enthusiastic, energetic and competitive. They are quick to anger but are strong of body.

**Yellow Aura:** Analytical, logical and brilliant. They are rational people who are happy with their company.

**Pink Aura:** Loving and caring. They like to be loved, but they are also very kind; people who like to give attention to anyone around them.

**Green Aura:** Creative, popular and respected. They have an eye for beautiful things, and they love to be in nature.

**Orange Aura:** Social and generous. They can sense the pain of others, and they like to help those who are in pain.

# Conclusion

An event such as opening your Third Eye Chakra is something you will know has happened. You will know because your intuition will never have felt so strong. You will instantly trust it and not question what you are told.

You will know that the wisdom you are seeing is very real and you will have no need to doubt it. Your Third Eye Chakra may not remain open. It may close down and leave you wondering where that clarity of thought disappeared to. This is because any part of your body can do that at any time dependent upon the way that you treat your body and the way you approach keeping that Chakra open.

For those who approach it in the same way as gaining something material, there will be a long wait. It isn't a material thing that you can switch on and off at will. In fact, if the basis of your life is materialism, you may find that you are unable to open that Chakra because you remain blocked by your inability to be humble.

The works that have been written over the years about the Chakras and the way forward are many. This book was written following an experience that was indeed extraordinary. It was my intention to share this experience through instruction so that others may draw closer to experiencing the wonders of the mind that may at this time lay dormant.

I wish you well with your journey and hope that you will be able to take this path and find your way. It is a matter of stepping from one steppingstone to the next, increasing your understanding as you go and gaining great spirituality from the voyage.

# Thank you!

Thank you again for purchasing this book!
I hope this book was able to help you get started with these amazing Techniques!

Finally, if you enjoyed this guide, then I´d like to ask you for a favor, would you be kind enough to leave a review for this book on Amazon?

Leaving a review allows me to improve it and good reviews mean the world to me.

70719801R00038

Made in the USA
Middletown, DE
16 April 2018